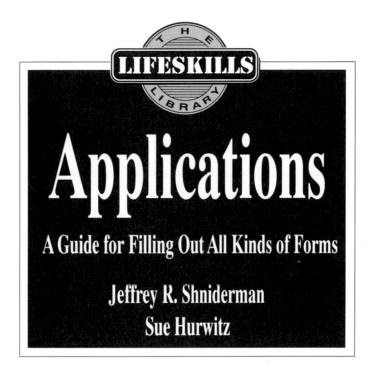

THE LIFESKILLS LIBRARY

Applications

A Guide for Filling Out All Kinds of Forms

Jeffrey R. Shniderman
Sue Hurwitz

THE ROSEN PUBLISHING GROUP, INC.

NEW YORK

In memory of my mother and father,
Alice and Paul Shniderman

Published in 1994 by The Rosen Publishing Group, Inc.
29 East 21st Street, New York, NY 10010

First Edition
Copyright 1994 by The Rosen Publishing Group, Inc.

Manufactured in the United States of America.

Library of Congress Cataloging-in-Publication Data

Shniderman, Jeffrey.
  Applications: a guide to filling out all kinds of forms / Jeffrey Shniderman and Sue Hurwitz
      p.   cm.   (The Life skills library)
  Includes bibliographical references and index.
  Summary: A guide to filling out such vital forms as applications for jobs, driver's license, social security, college admission, and credit cards, as well as health insurance and income tax forms, pointing out the necessity for knowing and keeping up-to-date records of one's personal data.
  ISBN 0-8239-1609-X
  1. Life skills—United States—Juvenile literature. 2. Business—United States—Forms—Juvenile literature. 3. Applications for positions—United States—Juvenile literature. 4. College applications—United States—Juvenile literature. [1. Life skills. 2. Applications for positions. 3. College applications.]
  I. Hurwitz, Sue, 1934–   II. Title. III. Series.
HQ2039.U6S55 1993
640—dc20   93-7911
                                                                  CIP
                                                                  AC

CONTENTS

INTRODUCTION

Applications and forms bring together information about you. All forms ask you to list personal information, or data. Your personal data show whether you meet certain requirements. Applications are written forms in which you ask for something.

On a driver's license application, your data show whether you are old enough for a license. On a job application, your data show your education, skills, and work experience. Employers use that information to decide whether you qualify for a job.

Many applications and forms ask for the same information. Common questions are your name, address, phone number, and social security number. You probably have these memorized. Some information you may not remember.

It is wise to be prepared. Make a list of your personal data. Take your list along to check with when you need to fill out forms. Read all the questions on the form before you begin to write. Think about your answers before you fill in the blanks. Print the information clearly.

This book tells about the personal data requested on some forms. It shows samples of forms. It helps you make your own personal data check.

Applications and forms provide specific personal information.

PERSONAL APPLICATIONS AND FORMS

Everyone who works needs a social security number. An employer uses your social security, or SS, number to send your tax money to your SS fund. Your employer also needs your SS number to report your earnings to the Internal Revenue Service. You use your social security number on your income tax return.

Parents need a social security number for children older than age one. Otherwise they cannot list the children as dependents on their income tax return.

If you are 18, apply in person at your nearest social security office for your SS number and card. You will fill out Form SS-5. The name you list should be the name on your birth certificate. You should not list a nickname.

You need proof of your age and identity. The SS office prefers your original birth certificate (not a photocopy) as proof. But you may use an original hospital record of your birth or of your baptism. You may also use a driver's license, a passport, or a school report card.

Your SS card is important. You keep the same SS number all your life. If you lose your card, you must fill out another SS-5 form. You must prove your age and identity with original records again.

John and Ross Apply for Social Security Cards

John met Ross at the local Social Security office. Both boys were waiting to apply for a social security number.

"Did you bring identification?" John asked Ross.

"I don't need to prove my identity," Ross bragged. "I got a social security card last year, but I lost it. Their computer will have my name in it."

"I called before I came over," John explained to Ross. "The clerk said you must have positive identification. She said it didn't matter if you had had a card before or not."

"What did you bring for identification?" Ross asked.

"I brought my birth certificate. I also have my driver's license with my picture on it." John heard a clerk call out the number 22. He glanced down to see that the number he held was next.

"I don't drive," Ross said. "I would use a driver's license for identification if I had one. But I'll talk them out of a new card anyway!"

John showed the clerk his completed SS-5 form and his birth certificate. He got a social security number and card. Ross argued and argued with the person who helped him. But he could not replace his social security card without proof of identity. Ross had wasted his trip to the Social Security office because he did not know the facts.

Driver's License Application

Driver's license applications are available at your state Driver License Examining Station. They include questions about your birthdate, residence, citizenship, physical impediments such as whether you wear glasses, and finally whether you want to donate your organs for transplant if you have a fatal accident. When you apply for your first license you must pass a driving test. An official rides with you to see if you are a safe driver.

Usually you must take a vision test to fulfill all the license requirements. Your eye doctor may sign your application instead if he has checked your vision within the last three months.

You must also pass a written test. The written driver's test asks questions about information explained in the driver's handbook. You may get this handbook from your driver's education class or from the Driver License Examining Station. You should study it.

The handbook discusses general driving rules. It shows pictures of traffic signals and traffic signs. Read the information beside these pictures carefully.

Most states have warnings on driver's license applications about driving under the influence of alcohol. Persons who hold a driver's license agree to take a chemical test for alcohol if they are ever arrested. Chemical tests may check the breath, blood, or urine. If a driver refuses to take these tests, he or she may have the driver's license taken away.

Drivers who are convicted of driving under the influence (DUI) may be fined. They may receive a jail sentence. Their driver's license may be suspended.

To renew a suspended driver's license, you must pass the written driver's test again. A handbook will be mailed to you shortly before your renewal date.

You must also pass another vision test. But you do not need to take another driving test unless you let your license expire.

Nora Applies for a Driver's License

Nora wanted to apply for a driver's license. Bess, Nora's older sister, drove her to the Driver License Examining Station. Bess waited in the car while Nora went in to fill out an application.

"You will need to pass a written test," the person in charge told Nora. "You may take one of these handbooks home. The handbook explains general driving rules and traffic signs. You should study it before taking the written test."

"Oh, I've been watching my parents and my sister drive for years," Nora replied. "I know what all the signs and signals mean. I don't need to study the handbook."

"It's your choice," the examiner said. "But if I were you, I'd look it over." He held out the handbook, practically putting it into her hand.

Nora sighed. She knew the examiner was probably right. But Bess had told her the test was easy. Bess had taught her to drive, and Bess thought she could pass it. Besides, she had winged tests before!

"I'm ready to take the test," Nora said firmly.

"Then go to the table by the window, and someone will help you."

Filling out an application is the first step to getting a driver's license.

The minute Nora saw the test, she was sorry she had not studied. She knew how to park and about speed limits. But there were several traffic signs she had never seen before. She knew she could not wing the written test.

And she was right.

"I can't believe you flunked the test," Bess complained as she drove home. "Now we'll have to make another trip back here."

"Sure, Bess. The test is easy for you. You've been driving for 10 years." Nora was so frustrated that she felt like crying. "There were pictures of signs on that test that I couldn't even guess at!"

Bess was quiet for a while. "I'm sorry, Sis. You're right. I shouldn't have advised you not to read the handbook. It was dumb to try to pass that test without studying for it."

Nora ignored the facts. She filled in the application for the driver's license. She listed her address, phone number, social security number, height, and weight.

But her application could not be processed until she had passed the written test and the driving test. If Nora had taken time to study, she surely would have passed the written test.

Nora took the handbook home. She read it over many times until she knew all the rules and signals. Several weeks later, Bess drove her back to the examining station. This time Nora passed the written test. She also passed the driving test. And Nora was able to drive Bess home.

College Applications

Applications for college enrollment are available at the Admissions Office of the college. This office also has applications for financial aid and information on the courses offered.

College applications ask for your educational history. They ask for the date of your high school graduation or general equivalency diploma (GED). They ask what other colleges you attended. These data are listed in chronological order. That is the order in which the events happened.

To list events in chronological order, start with the earliest events. For example, if you attended more than one high school, list your first high school. Then list your second high school. List the high school from which you graduated last.

Colleges ask you to supply a transcript, or record, of your grades and graduation. Your last school should mail your transcript directly to the college.

Most applications also ask you to list a major. Your major is the area of study in which you plan to take most of your classes. Some college applications list the majors offered and you check off one.

Many college applications ask for one or more personal references. References are people who know you and your ability and who will write a letter of recommendation for you.

You must supply all the information asked for on each application. If not, your application may be considered incomplete.

Application for Admission

Applicant Information

Maiden/Other Names

Middle

Date of Birth Mo./Day/Year

First

Sex: ☐ Male ☐ Female

ZIP

State

ZIP

Please Print
Name Last

Soc. Sec. # _____ - _____ - _____

Current Street Address   City

Permanent Street Address (if different from current)   City

( )
Evening Telephone Number

( )
Day Telephone Number

Relationship to Student

Evening Tel. Number

Person We May Contact in Case of an Emergency:

Last Name   First Name

Day Tel. Number

Street Address   City   State   ZIP

First Language: ☐ English ☐ Other _____
Ethnic Code* ☐ 1 Asi___ ___ ___ ☐ 2 Am. Indian or Alaskan Native ☐ 3 Black ☐ 4 Hispanic ☐ 5 Caucasian ☐ 6 Other ____
Disability* Type: _____
☐ Check here if you wish to have the Office of Special Services contact you regarding your needs and available services. You are not obligated to respond and if you do, ___ several federal and state statutes.

* This information i___
your responses ___

A. Citizenship:

B. Are you
1. On

2. I___
3.

Educational Information

High School

High School Name   City   State

Have you graduated from high school? ☐ No   Anticipated Date of Graduation: _____

Have you taken the GED? ☐ No ☐ Yes When? _____
Month / Year

☐ Yes _____
Month / Year

Office Use Only

If you have been out of high school less than five years and do not have 15 college credit hours, or if you are presently in high school, ask your high school to send an official transcript to Admissions and Records Office. Hand-carried copies are not acceptable.

College

List in chronological order all colleges attended

Name of college or university	Location (City and State)	Dates From Month/Year	To Month/Year	Credit Hours Earned	Degree Earned	Office Use Only

You are responsible for requesting that each school you have attended send an official transcript not be allowed to re-enroll after your first semester. If you are currently enrolled at another institution, have your transcript sent at the end of the semester with the current semester's grades included. Hand-carried copies are not acceptable.   If all transcripts are not submitted, you will

Educational Objectives

1. Are you seeking a degree or certificate   ☐ No ☐ Yes Please check the appropriate "program intent" in #3.
2. Check the one that best describes your current objective
☐ Transfer to another college/university   1
☐ Improve skills for present job
☐ Remedy or review basic skills   3
☐ Prepare to change careers   5
3. Program intent (Check only one)   7

☐ Prepare to enter job market   2
☐ Explore courses to decide on career   4
☐ Personal interest or self-improvement   6
☐ Undecided   8

Program Name

	Degree(s) Offered	Code
☐ Undecided (no major)		
☐ General Studies to transfer to college/university		
☐ Accounting	AA	99
☐ Administration of Justice		
☐ Automotive Repair	AT	10
☐ Automotive Technology	AA	40
☐ Aviation Maintenance Technology – Airframe	CP	12
☐ Aviation Maintenance Technology – Power Plant	AT	71
☐ Biomedical Equipment Technology	AT**	42
☐ Business Administration	AT**	02
☐ Chef Apprenticeship	AS	03
☐ Chemical Specialty	AT	20
☐ Civil Engineering Technology	AT	43
☐ Commercial Art	AS	44
☐ Computer Systems Technology	AT	49
☐ Data Processing	AT	21
☐ Data Processing – Mini/Micro	AS	45
☐ Data Processing, Advanced	AT	22
	CP	46
	CP	74
		70

☐ Data Processing, Computer Applic Technol   CP
☐ Dental Hygiene
☐ Drafting Technology – Civil   AS*   73
☐ Drafting Technology – Machine   AS   23
☐ Electronic Engineering Technology   AS   24
☐ Emergency Medical Science   AS   25
☐ Emergency Medical Technology   AS   27
☐ Emergency Services Dispatcher   AT   28
☐ Equine Studies   CP   48
☐ Fashion Merchandising   CP   76
☐ Fire Prevention   AT   77
☐ Fire Prevention   AS   51
☐ Fire Protection   AS   52
☐ Fire Protection   CP   30
☐ Fire Protection Administration   AS   79
☐ Heating, Ventilation and A/C   AS   31
☐ Heating, Ventilation and A/C   AS   80
☐ Hospitality Management   AT   32
☐ Hospitality Management   CP   50
☐ Information/Word Processing   AT   78
☐ Inform/Word Proc., Office Automation Technol   CP   53
     AT   82
     CP   55
     AT   87

☐ Interior Merchandising
☐ Interpreter Training
☐ Marketing and Management   AT   57
☐ Medical Records Technology   AT*   59
☐ Metal Fabrication   AT   62
☐ Mobile Intensive Care Technology   AT**   ___
☐ Nursing   CP   04
☐ Nursing   CP   85
☐ Occupational Therapy Assistant   AT   86
☐ Office Careers – Administrative Office Mgmt.   AA*   14
☐ Office Careers – Administrative Secretary   AS*   35
☐ Office Careers   AT   05
☐ Office Careers – Legal Secretary   AT   41
☐ Office Careers – Medical Secretary   CP   68
☐ Paralegal   AT   90
☐ Paralegal   AT   66
☐ Physical Therapy Assistant   AA   67
☐ Police Academy (for active duty officers only)   CP   64
☐ Radiology Technology   AT**   89
☐ Respiratory Therapy   CP   06
☐ Respiratory Therapy   CP   88
☐ Sales and Customer Relations   AS*   07
☐ Veterinary Technology   CP   37
     CP   91
     AT**   92
     AT**   01

AA = Associate of Arts (2-year degree program)
AS = Associate of Science (2-year degree program)
* These programs are "selective admission" programs. Additional requirements must be met for acceptance to these programs. If you are interested in one of these, notify the Admissions and Records Office as soon as possible.

AT =
CP =

Associate of Applied Science (2-year degree program)
Certificate Program (these programs vary from one semester to two years)

I certify that the information given is correct and complete. I understand that submission of false information and/or failure to submit supporting transcripts is grounds for denial of admission, re-enrollment or immediate suspension if enrolled. If accepted as a student I agree to abide by the rules and regulations of the college regarding conduct and other obligations. ____ does not print a student directory; however, student telephone numbers and addresses may be obtained at selected sites on campus. If you do not want others to have access to this information, contact the Admissions and Records Office.

Signature of Student _____

Date _____

Return your completed applications promptly to the Admissions Offices (deadlines are usually provided). Ask your high school to send a copy of your transcript to each school you have chosen. Be sure to include the correct application fee if the college requires one.

You should follow up your applications after about a month. Write or call the colleges to see if your transcripts, references, and fees were received.

Fay and Reba File College Applications

Fay and Reba were seniors in high school. They had several classes together. They ate lunch together every day. In the school lunchroom one day, they discussed their college applications.

"I just got an acceptance letter from my second choice," Fay announced.

"Great," Reba answered. "Why don't you seem happy?"

"I'd rather be accepted at my first-choice school," Fay said. "My cousin goes there, and I want to room with her."

"At least you heard from one college!" Reba answered. "That's better than I've done." She sighed. "How many applications did you send?"

"Five." Fay took a bite of her sandwich. "This waiting to hear back is the pits!"

"Tell me about it!" Reba groaned between mouthfuls of pizza. "I sent out seven applications and I haven't heard from any of them."

"Maybe you should write or call the schools you applied to. What if they didn't get all your data?" Fay asked. "I followed up on my applications. I found that I had forgotten to have a transcript sent to one of them."

Reba shrugged. "My grades aren't wonderful. That's probably why they aren't answering."

"Don't be so negative," Fay scolded. "You should follow up on those applications."

"I'll see," Reba answered. "It was enough of a hassle just getting them mailed out. I can't face any more paperwork right now."

Fay eventually heard from every college to which she applied. She was not accepted at three of them, but she *was* accepted at her first choice!

Reba waited several months before she followed up on her applications. She discovered that she had not asked for transcripts to be sent to four colleges. She also had not listed references on any of her applications. All her applications were incomplete. The colleges did not process them.

Reba stopped in her high school office and corrected her mistakes. But it was late. She was not accepted at any of the out-of-town colleges. Yet Reba was lucky. The local junior college still had space available, and she was accepted.

Reba learned the facts the hard way. When an application said, "Fill in completely," it meant it. Anything less was incomplete.

—

Fill out your college applications on a copy of the original form first. This gives you a chance to check your work.

Passport Application

If you plan to travel abroad, you need a United States passport. In foreign countries your passport is used for identification.

Most post offices have passport applications. U.S. passports are issued only to U.S. citizens or nationals. Applicants over 13 years of age must submit the completed application in person.

To get a passport, you need a completed application and proof of U.S. citizenship. You can see exactly what type of information is required on the sample application. You also need proof of identity, two identical photographs, and money for fees.

You may need to go to the main post office in your city or town to have your passport application processed.

Your birth certificate is proof of citizenship. You also may use hospital birth records or school records to prove your citizenship.

If the agent at the post office does not know you, your driver's license shows your signature and picture. It is proof of identity.

The photographs must have been taken in the last six months. They must be 2 x 2 inches in size. The pictures must be a front view of your face taken in street clothes without a hat or dark glasses.

If you are over 18, the passport fee is $55 plus a $10 execution fee. Your passport is valid, or good, for 10 years. If you are under 18, the passport fee is $30 plus the $10 fee. Your passport is valid for five years.

Bank Account Forms

There are several types of forms associated with bank accounts. The first is a simple application. To open a checking or savings account, you'll need to provide some basic information—your name, social security number, birthdate, and other items.

The next form you'll probably fill out is a deposit slip. When you put money into a bank, it is called a deposit. Your account number should always appear on your deposit slip to ensure that your money is put into the right account.

If you need your money to pay bills, deposit it in a checking account. Money is taken, or withdrawn, from your account when a check you write is cashed. Most banks require a minimum amount of money, or balance, in checking accounts. Otherwise, they charge a service fee.

Deposit money that you do not need to spend immediately in a savings account. Your money earns more interest in a savings account than in an interest-paying checking account. Money is safe in a bank, especially if it is an FDIC bank. That means your money is protected by the Federal Deposit Insurance Corporation.

You fill out a bank deposit slip when you put money into a bank. A bank deposit slip has rows and columns to list the kind of money you deposit. One space says CASH. This space may be divided into CURRENCY (paper money) and COIN (dimes, quarters, etc.). The deposit slip also has spaces to list each check separately.

You must endorse, or sign, a check made out to you when you deposit it. Sign your name on the back of the check on the left-hand side. Sign your name exactly as it is written on the face of the check. If your name is misspelled, sign it twice.

21

First sign it as it is written on the check, then sign it correctly. Many banks also ask you to write your account number under your endorsement.

The bank gives you a receipt for your deposit. Check the deposit amount and your account number carefully to make sure they are correct. Save your deposit receipts in the back of your checkbook.

Once a month the bank sends you a statement. This statement shows your bank balance. Your balance is the amount of money in your account after all charges and checks have cleared. Your canceled checks and deposit slips are sent with the statement.

Write checks carefully. First fill in the check stub, or register. On the register, write the date, the check number, the amount, and the name of the person or company to whom you write the check.

Write on the check the date, the name of the person or company, and the amount of the check both in numbers and in words. Then sign the check. If your account number or check number are not printed on the check, write those in, too.

Do not leave blank spaces that could be used to change the amount of your check. Write the amount in figures close to the dollar sign. Start writing the amount in words close to the left-hand side. These two amounts must agree. If there is a question about the amount of your check, the amount written in words is the one accepted. If your check is for less than one dollar, cross out the word "Dollars" and write "Only ___ cents."

Withdrawal forms are used to withdraw, or to take out money, from a savings account. Withdrawal forms are similar to checks. They are filled out in the same way. You must go to your bank to use a withdrawal form. The money you withdraw can be given to you in cash, a bank check, or a money order. Or sometimes you may want to transfer money from your savings account to your checking account. That can be done, too.

Bonnie and Bruce Open Bank Accounts

Bonnie and Bruce were twins. Their mother had a full-time job. During the school year both Bonnie and Bruce helped their mom around the house. They fixed dinner and did the laundry. They studied hard to make good grades at school.

Bonnie and Bruce earned a little money doing odd jobs. Bonnie baby-sat, and Bruce mowed lawns and shoveled snow.

The summer after they turned 16, they both got real jobs. Bonnie sold baby clothes in a store, and Bruce helped a neighbor paint houses. They now had more money than they needed, so they opened savings accounts. "Besides," their mother said, "your money will be safer in a bank than laying around your rooms."

On their 18th birthday, Bruce complained, "My savings account is a nuisance! It's such a bother to have to go to the bank every time I need money for something. "

"Well," his mom said, "now that you're both 18 you can have your own checking accounts. Then you can write a check when you want to buy something big, or pay a bill."

"That'll be great," Bonnie chimed in. "If I see something special, I can buy it without having to go to the bank."

"You'll need to keep good records, " their mom warned, "You'll need to keep track of every check you write. Othererwise you may spend more money than you have in your account. Then the bank won't honor your check and it will bounce. You'll be charged 10 to 20 dollars for a service fee!"

"Not to mention the embarrassment of facing someone to whom you gave a rubber check!" Bruce added.

"I'll be careful, Mom," Bonnie promised. "I'm not about to pay out my hard-earned money on unnecessary charges!"

Bonnie and Bruce opened checking accounts the following week. Bonnie filled out her check register for every check before she wrote it.

Bruce was better at details than his sister. He had no problem remembering to fill in his register for each check. He also compared his bank balance with his monthly statement to be sure the statement agreed with the amount in his checkbook.

Bonnie had no problem using her checking account during the summer when she worked.

Opening a bank account is easy. A bank employee will expain the details and answer any questions you may have.

Because she didn't write many checks, Bonnie didn't usually bother checking her bank statements.

At the end of August, Bonnie quit her job to get ready for school. She bought some new jeans and a couple of sweaters. She bought school supplies. She wrote a check at the pizza parlor when she ate out with her friends. After school started, Bonnie was busy with her homework.

"I think this overdraft notice is for you," Bruce teased one day when he brought in the mail. "Someone hasn't been balancing her checkbook!"

Bonnie had to pay a $20 overdraft charge. But because the amount of the check was small, the bank honored it. Bonnie was thankful she wouldn't have to cringe every time she went to the pizza parlor. Now Bonnie knew the facts. She watched her checking account carefully.

Credit Card Application

Credit card companies enable you to make purchases, or buy things, with a charge card and pay for them later. Credit card companies give you credit. They do not give you free money! You must pay for everything you charge on a credit card.

Credit card applications are all very similar. They ask where you are employed. They ask your annual income and any debts you may owe. They ask for your bank account numbers so they can check with your bank. They use this information to see if you can afford to pay your bills.

Applicant's Name			
Street Address		State	Zip Code
City		Social Security Number	
Home Phone Number ( )	☐ Self-Employed †	Position	Date of Birth
Employer	Business Phone ( )		Annual Income $
Years Employed			Years There
Previous Address		Your Bank	☐ CHECKING ☐ SAVINGS
Residence Information ☐ RENT ☐ OWN ☐ LIVE WITH RELATIVES			Relationship
Name of Nearest Relative Not Living With You			
Relative's Address (Street)			Phone
City/State/Zip			

Co-Applicant Information

This section should be completed if you are applying for a joint account or relying on another person's income

Co-Applicant's Name		Date of Birth	Business Phone
Social Security Number			Annual Income $
		Years Employed	Position
	☐ Employed †		

Some credit card applications ask for co-applicants who also will be responsible for your charges. Sometimes a relative will agree to cosign the application to help you quality for a card.

There are many credit card companies. Some of the bigger companies are Visa, American Express, MasterCard, and Discover.

Most credit card companies charge an annual, or yearly, membership fee. Some companies allow a one-month grace period, or interest-free period, in which to pay your bill. Some companies start charging interest the minute your purchase is made.

Most credit card companies charge a high rate of interest on unpaid balances. They also charge a high rate of interest on bills paid late. Many credit cards allow you to charge a cash advance on your credit card. They charge a fee for this transaction.

Credit card companies list *disclosures* on the application. Disclosures explain the company's charges for its services. Disclosures often are printed in small type. You need to read them carefully.

Some people are careless with credit cards. They charge more than they can afford. They pay their bills late, or not at all. These people get bad credit ratings. They will have trouble getting credit in the future.

Be careful how you use a credit card. If you charge purchases, pay your bills on time. That will help you keep a good credit rating.

Federal Income Tax Forms

Everyone who earns money must pay a federal tax on that income. Your employer withholds a percentage of your wages for this tax. The number of dependents, or people whom you support, affects the amount of money that is withheld. Your employer sends this money to the Internal Revenue Service (IRS). The money deposited for you during the year becomes a tax credit when you file your tax return.

In January, your employer sends you a W-2 form. It shows the amount of money you earned during

---

Many new products come with a warranty card. For your own protection, fill out the card and return it to the manufacturer as soon as possible.

BE SURE TO FILL
OUT AND
RETURN THIS
WARRANTY
CARD.

Department of the Treasury—Internal Revenue Service

Form **1040EZ**

Income Tax Return for
Single Filers With No Dependents (L)

OMB No. 1545-0675

Name & address

Use the IRS label (see page 10). If you don't have one, please print.

L
A
B
E
L

Print your name (first, initial, last)

H
E
R
E

Home address (number and street). (If you have a P.O. box, see page 11.) | Apt. no.

City, town or post office, state, and ZIP code. (If you have a foreign address, see page 11.)

Please print your numbers like this:

9 8 7 6 5 4 3 2 1 0

Your social security number

Please see instructions on the back. Also, see the
Form 1040EZ booklet.

Presidential Election Campaign (see page 11)
Do you want $1 to go to this fund?

Note: Checking "Yes" will not change your tax or reduce your refund. ▶

Yes No

Dollars   Cents

Report your income

1 Total wages, salaries, and tips. This should be shown in Box 10 of your W-2 form(s). (Attach your W-2 form(s).)   1

Attach Copy B of Form(s) W-2 here. Attach tax payment on top of Form(s) W-2.

2 Taxable interest income of $400 or less. If the total is more than $400, you cannot use Form 1040EZ.   2

3 Add line 1 and line 2. This is your **adjusted gross income**.   3

Note: *You* **must** *check Yes or No.*

4 Can your parents (or someone else) claim you on their return?
   ☐ **Yes.** Do worksheet on back; enter amount from line E here.
   ☐ **No.** Enter 5,550.00. This is the total of your standard deduction and personal exemption.   4

5 Subtract line 4 from line 3. If line 4 is larger than line 3, enter 0. This is your **taxable income.**   5

Figure your tax

6 Enter your Federal income tax withheld from Box 9 of your W-2 form(s).   6

7 **Tax.** Use the amount on **line 5** to find your tax in the tax table on pages 16-18 of the booklet. Enter the tax from the table on this line.   7

Refund or amount you owe

8 If line 6 is larger than line 7, subtract line 7 from line 6. This is your **refund.**   8

9 If line 7 is larger than line 6, subtract line 6 from line 7. This is the **amount you owe.** Attach your payment for full amount payable to the "Internal Revenue Service." Write your name, address, social security number, daytime phone number, and "1991 Form 1040EZ" on it.   9

Sign your return

I have read this return. Under penalties of perjury, I declare that to the best of my knowledge and belief, the return is true, correct, and complete.

For IRS Use Only — Please do not write in boxes below.

the previous year. You must fill out one of the many tax return forms. Mail the W-2 and your tax return to the IRS by April 15 each year.

Form 1040EZ is for single persons with no dependents. This form asks for your total, or gross, income. That includes wages, salaries, tips, and all other money you received during the year.

Each year, the IRS mails you a Form 1040, Form 1040A, or Form 1040EZ, depending on which return you filed the year before. They include instructions. If you do not receive a tax return package in the mail, you may call 1-800-TAX-FORM (1-800-829-3637).

You can get tax forms and instruction booklets at many libraries between January and April each year. Some libraries have video tapes of tax return instructions in English or Spanish. Volunteers also help you fill out your tax return form.

The Internal Revenue Service examines income tax returns. If you fail to report your income correctly you may be notified by the IRS even several years later. You may have to pay a high penalty fee plus the amount you did not report. If you are untruthful on purpose or swear falsely about your reported income, you commit perjury. Then you could be sent to prison.

You may also need to file a state income tax return. These forms vary from state to state, but they are similar to the federal income tax returns.

You should keep a copy of your income tax returns and your W-2 forms for at least seven years. Also keep all receipts and cancelled checks to prove amounts you claim as deductions or credits. It is wise to keep a note of the date you filed your return.

Ted and Clayton File Income Tax Returns

Ted got a summer job at a fast-food restaurant. He met Clayton, who also worked there. Ted was 16, and Clayton was 18. This was Ted's first job, and

Clayton showed him the ropes. The boys soon became friends.

After school started, Ted worked only on weekends. But Clayton had dropped out of school. He still worked full time.

"Did you get your W-2 form yet?" Clayton asked Ted one day in January.

"I got it yesterday," Ted answered. They stood behind the counter waiting for customers. "I guess I'll file my income tax return right away."

"Why sweat it?" Clayton asked as he adjusted his cap. "You've got until April 15."

Ted sighed. "It won't be any easier later. I'd rather do it now and have it over with!"

"Suit yourself," Clayton replied. "Filing income tax returns isn't a high priority for me. I put it off until the last minute."

The following week Ted went to the library to do research for a school report. He asked the librarian if the library had tax return booklets.

"Sure," the librarian replied. "They are on the table by the copy machine. There is information on how to fill out the forms, too."

"Thanks," said Ted.

"If you need help, one of our volunteers will gladly answer your questions."

Ted nodded. He would try to figure out the tax forms on his own. But if he did get frustrated, he would ask for help.

—

Anyone over the legal working age must report their income to the federal government by preparing a tax return each year.

"I mailed off my 1040EZ today," Ted told Clayton the following weekend. "Boy, I'm glad to have that behind me! Have you filed your return yet?" he asked, making conversation.

"I'm getting there. I worked at three jobs last year, so I have three W-2 forms to file," Clayton complained. "I already lost one of them."

"Can't you get a copy from your employer?"

"I guess so." Clayton shrugged. "He fired me, so I hate to ask for a favor."

"You'll need that W-2 for your tax return," Ted answered. "You'd better ask."

"No sweat," Clayton said. "I'll handle it when the time comes."

Ted was a little anxious about filing his first income tax return. But he knew the facts. He had to do it. Ted learned all he could at the library. He read all the directions carefully. Then he filled in his 1040EZ. Before he mailed it, he showed the form and his W-2 to his dad. Ted gave a sigh of relief when his dad said it was correct.

Clayton never bothered to get his missing W-2 forms. He filed his income tax return with only two of the three forms. He didn't know the facts. He didn't know that he would have to pay a fine when the IRS checked his records. Some months later the IRS caught the mistake. Clayton was sent a bill for the taxes due on the missing W-2 form and also a large fine. As if that was not bad enough, Clayton now had more paperwork, too!

JOB APPLICATIONS
AND FORMS

Take your personal data checklist when you apply for a job. It will help you to be accurate. Read all directions carefully before you begin. Write neatly in ink.

Most applications ask for the same information:

1. Your legal name, address, and phone number. (You also need the name and phone number of someone to call in an emergency.)

2. Your social security number.

3. The name or title of the job for which you are applying.

4. Education information. All the schools you attended and the date you graduated. Start with the first school and move to the most recent. Use a telephone book to find the addresses of your schools if you do not know them.

5. Your work history. Include specific dates of employment and the kind of work you did.

6. The names and addresses of several people who know you or your work, for references. Teachers or former employers are good people to ask. Get their correct titles, telephone numbers, and addresses, and always ask their permission first.

7. You may be asked to list special skills, talents, and hobbies. You should also include any honors and awards received in your school or community.

8. Fill in all the blanks. If a question does not apply to you, write N/A or NA (for Not Applicable). Or write "No" or "None."

Résumé

Résumé is a French word that means "summary." A résumé is a summary of your education, training, skills, and work history. Most résumés are one page long. The information for your résumé is on your personal data list. It is information requested on many job applications.

Your résumé should have a heading that includes your name, address, city, state, and phone number. It can be centered near the top of the page.

Study the sample résumé. Notice that it has several other headings on the left-hand side of the page. *Education*: Your present high school grade

—

A neat résumé is important. Use a typewriter or computer for your final version.

or graduation date. If you have any college credits, they should be listed also. *Work History*: Any jobs you have held. If this will be your first job, list any volunteer jobs that show experience.

Your résumé should be typed or printed neatly. You should use white paper. If you make copies, be sure they look professional. If you cannot get a good, clear photocopy, use only originals.

Laura and Elaine Apply for a Job

Laura and Elaine both applied for a job at a hardware store. Laura filled in the job application. She wrote her social security number in the correct place. She had never worked before, so she wrote N/A in the space that asked for her work history. Elaine had brought a résumé. It showed that she had mowed lawns and done baby-sitting for three years.

The manager called both girls into his office. "You have some work experience, Elaine," he said, looking up from her application. "It shows that you can handle responsibility. But I cannot hire you here without a social security number. Come back after you get one."

Then he turned to Laura. "I see by your application that you pay attention to details. You do not have any experience, but you can be trained on the job. At least you have a social security number. I need someone to work as soon as possible. Can you start working this afternoon?"

Application for Employment

Our policy is to provide equal employment opportunity to all qualified persons without regard to race, creed, color, religious belief, sex, age, national origin, ancestry, physical or mental handicap or veteran status.

First _____ Middle _____ Date _____

Name – Last _____ State _____ Zip _____

Street Address _____ Social Security # _____

City _____

Telephone ( ) _____

Position applied for _____ Desired Wage $ _____

How did you hear of this opening? _____

When can you start? _____

Are you a U.S. citizen or otherwise authorized to work in the U.S. on an unrestricted basis? ☐ Yes ☐ No

Are you looking for full time employment? ☐ Yes ☐ No

If no, what hours are you available? _____ Are you willing to work graveyard? ☐ Yes ☐ No

Are you willing to work swing shift? ☐ Yes ☐ No

Do you have a physical or medical condition which would limit your capacity for the job applied for? ☐ Yes ☐ No

If yes, please describe the condition and explain the work limitations.

_____

_____

_____

Have you ever been convicted of a felony? ☐ Yes ☐ No

If yes, please describe conditions. _____

Year   Major   D

Laura got her job because she was prepared. She filled in the job application neatly. She did not leave any blank spaces. She was able to supply a social security number. Elaine did not have a social security number. She wasted her time applying for a job she could not start.

Doctor and Health Insurance Forms

When you visit a doctor for the first time you fill in a health history form. These forms usually have a list of health problems. You check off the health problems you have had.

It is helpful to make a personal health checklist before you leave home. Ask a parent which childhood diseases you had and the dates. Ask what immunizations, or shots, you have had. Your school records show your immunizations if you need more help. It is important that your health history be as accurate as possible. That helps the doctor to give you better care.

Your doctor keeps a record of your visits. This record includes any health problem and the recommended treatment. When you apply for health insurance, the insurance company asks permission to see these records.

Health insurance forms ask the name of your primary-care physician. That is the doctor who usually treats you. The forms ask about previous illnesses. They ask what medicines you take. They ask if you use tobacco or drugs, or if you have AIDS. Here, too, a health checklist is useful.

Health insurance forms ask if you are applying for coverage just for yourself or for a family. They ask which deductible you want. A deductible is the amount of money you agree to pay for medical bills. This amount is subtracted from your total medical bills. The insurance company pays a percentage of the balance. Usually, the higher the amount of the deductible, the lower your premium, or monthly charge, will be.

———

The medical information that you provide for your doctor is very important. This health history becomes part of your permanent medical record.

SUMMARY

Forms and applications are important. They tell people something about you. You should fill them in with care. Your information should be accurate.

Make a personal data list if you do not have one. Use your list to fill in forms and applications. That will keep your information accurate.

Keep good records of your personal data. Keep a record of your social security number. Keep a record of your bank account numbers. If you apply for college admission or a job, keep a record of each application. You should also record the date you ordered a transcript sent to each college. *Always* keep a copy of your income tax return.

Keep yourself organized. Put together a personal file of all your important papers.

Your medical history is a record that you will need all your life. If you apply for health insurance or enter a hospital, you need this information.

In the early years of your working life, you will probably change jobs several times. You may find that the kind of work you have chosen does not really suit you. You may get a chance to move to a job with a higher pay and better opportunity for advancement. In these years keep careful records of your jobs: the dates, the duties, your supervisor, and the reason for leaving. You will need this information on later job applications.

Keep your lists accurate. It takes only a minute to update your lists. Keep them in a place where you can find them. Your personal data lists help keep your information organized.

GLOSSARY
EXPLAINING NEW WORDS

applicant A person who applies for something.

chronological order The order in which things happened.

contribution Money, knowledge, or something that you give.

deductible The amount you must pay before your insurance company pays a claim.

FICA Federal Insurance Contributions Act, which allows Social Security taxes to be withheld from paychecks.

Form 1040EZ The income tax form to use if you are single and do not want to list deductions.

IRS Internal Revenue Service, the agency that collects federal income taxes.

national A citizen or subject of a country.

personal data list A written summary of important facts about your education and work history.

résumé A summary of education and work experience used mostly to find employment.

Social Security Administration The federal agency that collects Social Security taxes from your wages. It pays you benefits if you become disabled or when you retire.

transcript A printed copy of your school records.

W-2 Form A wage and tax statement of the amount of money an employee earned for the year.

FOR FURTHER READING

Anthony, Rebecca, and Roe, Gerald. *Finding a Job in Your Field*. Princeton, NJ: Peterson's Guides, 1984.

Coxford, Lola M. *Résumé Writing Made Easy,* 3rd ed. Scottsdale, AZ: Gorsuch Scarisbrick Publishers, 1989.

Evicci, Fred W. *The New Social Security Guide*. Sacramento, CA: Capital Publications, 1989.

Levy, Joan U. and Norman. *College Admissions: A Handbook for Students and Parents*. New York: Simon & Schuster, 1988.

Lipman, Burton E. *The Professional Job Search Program*. New York: John Wiley & Sons, 1983.

Littrell, J.J. *From School to Work*. South Holland, IL: Goodheart-Willcox Co., 1991.

Moreau, Daniel. *Take Charge of Your Career*. Washington, DC: Kiplinger Books, 1990.

Yate, Martin John. *Résumés That Knock 'em Dead*. Holbrook, MA: Bob Adams, Inc., 1988.

INDEX

48

APPLICATIONS

About the Authors

Jeffrey R. Shniderman has a degree in business. In his job as a regional sales manager for a food distributor, he works daily with all kinds of forms and applications.

Sue Hurwitz has taught school for many years. She is also coauthor of *Drugs and Your Friends, Hallucinogens, Drugs and Birth Defects*, and *Staying Healthy*.

Photo Credits
Cover: Dru Nadler
All photos by Dru Nadler except page 37: Stuart Rabinowitz.

Design & Production: Blackbirch Graphics, Inc.